IN THE
THAW
OF DAY

poems by

Cynthia Good

Finishing Line Press
Georgetown, Kentucky

IN THE
THAW
OF DAY

In The Thaw of Day is dedicated to my sons Alden and Julien Reiman; my brothers Glendon and Brad and dear friends who helped me through and believed in me; Meg Reggie, Keiko Drew, Susan Johnson, Barbara Barry, Tina Good, Jill Campbell, Christine Leuthold, Danica Kombol, Maria Guarisco and Albert Amato, Denise Direnzo, Monica Diaz Rivera, Dawn Solomon, Genevive Pelletier, Kathy Hart, Trina Keuller, Sacy Bryant, Annette Loper, Rob Brinson; my poetry community Ann Buxie, Nathan Hassall, Heidi Seaborn, Karen Javits, Kathryn Kelly; to the extraordinary humans and poets I've had the chance to learn from and who made me realize I wasn't crazy, I just needed this language; Catherine Barnett, Camille Dungy, Memye Curtis Tucker, Mathew Rohrer, Robin Coste Lewis, Nick Laird, Brian Teare, Brenda Hillman, Victoria Chang, Deborah Landau, Forrest Gander; and especially this is dedicated to my editor and friend and wonderful poet Travis Denton.

Publisher: Leah Huete de Maines

Editors: Christen Kincaid and Travis Denton

Cover Art: Elaine Marinoff Good, *The Dawn on Sam's Creek*

Author Photo: Rob Brinson

Cover Design: Elizabeth Maines McCleavy and Travis Denton

Order online: www.finishinglinepress.com
also available on amazon.com

Author inquiries and mail orders:
Finishing Line Press
PO Box 1626
Georgetown, Kentucky 40324
USA

Contents

A thinking woman sleeps with monsters.
The beak that grips her, she becomes.

~ Adrienne Rich

The Striped Marlin We Set Free

We trolled fast from harbor to Chileno Bay looking
for dorados and landed a striped marlin, her satin skin
a negligee of streaming gold, indigo and green,
her elegant bill, a sword but useless in the struggle.
She flailed hard, drumming the hollow fiberglass,
heaving her slim self into a corner, torso arching,
hammering with all she had. Imagine her surprise
as ocean flooded her eyes, a hook ripping into her
lip. We felt her in our chairs where we sat watching
her stomp and snake her midsection. She thrashed
like she knew what we wanted to do to her, battering
the only thing she had, banging her body into boat.
I steadied against the pitch and felt her thump
the scorching deck, diesel burning our noses. I saw
her stunned-wide eyes. She pounded like she knew
if she lost we would tear her open, a dull knife
slicing into a burger, cut like fabric, like she knew
we'd carve her into pieces, maybe eat her alive
as my father and I did after catching tuna, like she
knew once dead, we'd hoist her up to weigh our
trophy, knew we'd laugh and high five
with our grimy salt-crusted hands, glistening
with her scales as they caught the spinning sun,
like she knew we'd hose down the deck, diluting
her burgundy, flushing away any sign of her,
until there'd be no evidence we were ever there.

My Father's Smoke

There was the crinkling
cellophane, then pulling
the gold strip to open
the five packs he puffed
each day. Did it relax him
exhaling the stylish toke?

Or did it burn him
as he lit up each morning
before flipping on the light?
I was addicted to his
balm of Salem Menthol
masking everything bad—

stuffy bedrooms, stench
of diesel fuel and sea
sickness. Their shouts
from the kitchen. I would
stub out his cigarette
decades before we
suspected emphysema,

the only time I recall
him yelling at me.
I savor the aroma.
Even now, all of him
in the ocean—
if someone lights up
I inch in to get closer.

My Elephant Tree

With less than a dozen days of rain
each year, the trees and shrubs are silver

as bone. The desert here in the Tropic
of Cancer looks like an old woman

I saw at the doctor's office, like her mist
blue hair and gnarled fingers. The golden

Torote's papery skin rips away between
my fingers. But it doesn't collapse

as I thought. It is agile as a new leaf.
When I bend it, it doesn't snap. It arches

all the way back before it breaks, and now
I see the life inside it as I inhale its eucalyptus,

the source of frankincense and myrrh. All
these plants are perfume and quietly alive

and waiting for the rain that comes
in the fall, waiting for someone to notice.

Voices in My Head
While Trying to Sleep, Sunday Night

Got to call Dr. W in the morning for refill.
Where's that half Ambien. Up/Look for,
but don't find half Ambien. Down/Need
to call N tomorrow. Wonder if she's avoiding
me. Need to call V. Is she avoiding me. Up/

Check phone messages. Down/Remember
not to worry about the outcome, like getting
lost tonight driving home without glasses
under shadows of huge trees, big
as mountains, a smattering of moonlight,

a tunnel of monsters around me. Up/Why's
the dog at the bottom of the bed. Down/
The bookshelf fits perfectly on the other wall.
Got to stop the *Times* while I'm out of town.
Up/Midnight. Down/Check on D to see if she

is still a wreck like S who gets drunk
and sleeps with random men. Up/Wonder
am I doing that too, but with one random man?
Down/Got to order vibrator. Up/Drag dog
closer. Growls. Crawls back to bottom of bed.

Down/The vibrator my friend suggested
is $100. I'm worth it. *You can't have the life
that's waiting for you if you keep living the life
you have,* Joseph Campbell said that, I think.
I'm a fuck up. I am doing a good job.

Up/2:30AM. Pull the dog closer.
She growls and barks. Apply Chapstick.
Down/Dammit. Take five deep breaths, fill
stomach first. Up/On the fifth, let the air drift
out of mouth. Try to imagine god holding me.

Down/Remember Step 11, …*pray only
for knowledge of god's will.* Try to stop
trying. Up/Adjust pillow. Down/Fuck.
Too late to get a good night's sleep.
I wish it was morning, so I could shut off

my fucking brain. Up/Wait. I love you brain.
Thank you, brain. Down/The dog is now sleeping
against my side, pink streaks the sky, streetlights
flicker off, birds quiet the crickets, and the starred
darkness climbs under a blanket of growing light.

The Nature of Monogamy

The bald eagle, the oldfield mouse,
the albatross, and Atlantic puffin

who spends time at sea after breeding—
these guys lodge together for life.

Coyotes are known to never cheat
like gibbons, the seahorse and lovebirds.

But don't believe it about lovebirds.
It's true mine were thrust together,

plucked from a Petco. An unsuccessful
arranged marriage, they bickered

nonstop like a broken wheel,
a squeaky door hinge, tennis shoes

grinding a basketball court. Then
one of the birds died. The other

lives happily, unlike titi monkeys
who *exhibit signs of distress* when

away from the other, says Citizens
for the Preservation of Wildlife.

I can't blame them or fairytales
that I want a prince on his white

fucking horse to rescue me
from my self-loathing. Geese

protect their mates from predators,
as do barn owls and swans.

The prairie vole, poster child
of animal monogamy, stays true

even after death, 80 percent
of the time. My friend Arlette

once said of a divorcee, *Of course
she's alone. Who would want her?*

But Arlette's husband, I know,
is a cheater and fall-down drunk.

Ninety percent of birds and five
percent of mammals mate for life—

gray wolves, black vultures,
French angelfish, the scarlet macaw,

California condor. During a recent
breakup, Person-X told me,

You are too beautiful to be alone,
but all I could think of was how

the sandhill crane, shingleback
lizard and octopus stay true for life,

and the beaver too—at least until
one dies, then the other moves on.

Recuerdo

Not the blooming plumeria reflecting off the water,

the full moon this morning falling out of the sky,
not my hair, well maybe some,

not my strong muscles or breasts, smooth skin, youthful

and mid-life beauty, not even my breath or this house,
its walls, this car, the awesome

tires, plants in the garden that I water and trim.

But I can keep the ocean, sky and moon, dirt and air and space
between my cells, but not

the whales, not the bats that bolt from Mexico in winter.

I can keep the animal part of me, sternum, scapula, clavicle,
the part that notices bits of clouds gathering together like lace

in the northern sky waiting to dissolve, the chance to rest

on a featherless pillow, and nap
on the veranda Friday at noon, the part that insists

on standing in the shade to escape the heat or rifling through

the calendar growing thinner
in my fingers, as the dog races around with her blue ball,

its light flashing like an ambulance.

After the Hurricane, Witch Moth

When the storm went quiet
the witch moth came, her delicate
wings folding and unfolding
like a wedge of geese, like a raincoat,
unfolding like darkness, like grief.
Her wings quavered like violin strings,
mountain brave and foolish as I had been,
rushing, but too late to attach storm shutters.

Dark as velvet, edged in lace,
near the size of a bat, her wings twitched
like smudges of ash or abandoned
prayer, a harbinger of luck, or death
some say if she ducks into every corner
of your house. She fluttered around
the pantry, gazelle-like, draped
on a lime squeezer, a flickering

hand shadow puppet. She
arrived after the hurricane flipped
heavy wooden chairs, ripped doors
off the shed, twisted the almond tree
sideways as we cocooned in the pantry
listening to the rattling windows arch
against the wind. In a blog I read
on witch moths, a woman in Ohio said,

*"I felt I was seeing God. I cried
for hours."* When the sun returned,
I washed the loads of towels, dragged
furniture back outside, swept glass,
returned pillows to their chairs
until my arms ached from the rush
of the squall, then silence, like the earth
stunned in its tracks. This morning,

I found one black wing,
length of my hand, crisp as parchment
on the atrium floor, another under the lip
of the kitchen sink, no other sign of her,
just the video I took, the dog and I
gazing up at this creature
who survived the gale, a life more
evolved, who knew when to stay still.

Bats flood the sky here at dusk,

black sparks in the failing blue light
over the Pacific. Till now, I mistook them

for erratic birds. 1,400 species, ranging
in size from bumblebee to flying fox
with a 6-foot wingspan, a symbol

some say of death and rebirth
depending on who you ask. Most eat
their body weight in insects each night.

Seeing them warns of ruin if you go
with the bible. I am amazed
at their full speed ahead confidence

as they amble like drunk drivers
away from the sun, three-inch tongues
feeding on nectar and spreading

seeds from nuts and figs. Others say
they signify letting go of the past,
like chipped paint. I am drawn

to the fury above us, bats peppering
the sky, rummaging for scorpions
and mosquitos, avoiding daylight.

God of death in the Mayan culture,
and the luckiest animal in Macedonia,
the only mammal who flies, licks itself

clean as a cat. And they do not care
or know about symbols—instead
they sleep, woven upside down

together in crevices of rocks
and dead trees. Some fly
over 100 miles an hour and live

more than 40 years, I learn as a cloud
of them flickers above me, so quiet
I nearly miss their fluttering wings.

Theory of Object Permanence

The clock tells me
I've spent too much time
sleeping. The painting tells me
my mother is dead, my mother,
the painter, is dead and so are the lovers
in her painting, the pink curled
limbs spilling around one another.
They never really lived. My mother
in the painting with the man
she loved, lived. In the painting,
they are living now. The Eiffel Tower
souvenirs on the shelf tell me
I cannot go to Paris; they tell me
I remember Paris, and how
the wind off the Seine
crawls under your scarf. The black
and white photo from the museum,
an image of Basquiat between us
tells me Basquiat is dead,
and in this photo, all of us are memory.

Lentiformis Mesencephali

This enables a hummingbird to move in any direction with
equal agility.
—Audubon.org

They come to the feeder every day
      though it's empty. They tack
their little beaks into the vacant red
      metal flowers, look right,

then left, and take off. Near the deck
      above Tivoli Cove the pelicans
glide an inch over their shadows,
      always in groups, crows

in couples, adjacent in the palm tree
      at eyelevel, a dove alone
on the banister. I see the feeder
      swaying now in the breeze

which reminds me of my own
      dancing, which makes
everything in front of me like rain
      on a window. I want to

be more like a scientist who studies
      these birds to build better
robots, helicopters and drones
      because of the hummingbird's

brain, size of a rice grain, wings
      moving faster than an F15
eagle. They make *Instantaneous*
      course corrections,

while my brain, smaller compared
        to my body, can't remember
to close the garage door. One
        looks at me and darts off,

a reminder to fill the feeder as
        others fly around like sparks,
like a teacher's scolding finger,
        like jewels catching the sun.

East Cape, Baja CA

What am I that I should love
so wisely and so well?
          —Edna St. Vincent Millay, from *The Philosopher*

What are you to own a room inside me,
you who said, *The more bruised you are*
the better. And when I reeled

in that swordfish, you told me, *Catch it*
like a man. I wrote you a letter, the one
you write and never send,

and I sent it. And I didn't see you again.
This weekend I collected leggy limbs
of driftwood, pitted and ribbed

with spines, silver from waves and baptism
by sun. I've placed those sticks in a broken
pot I couldn't use for much else,

in a corner of the room I always notice.
What are you to still live, your edges round
and sharp and even now though I only see

you in grainy photos. What are you
to occupy my mind, you who everyone
worshiped like Independence Day,

going a million miles a minute until
you came to a standstill. And what am I,
frayed and rigid like those limbs,

and thinking I've loved wisely and well,
as the late afternoon high tide takes
the sticks it wants and disregards the rest.

My Father's Father

My father kept a sepia tone photo, he and his father,
their fingers intertwined around lines hooked

with bleeding fish, my father's chest thrust out,
chin up, his shoulders against his father's waist,

smiling like the horizon. Both of them quiet
and elusive like my father was to me. But he

taught me to fish as a girl. Like he did with his
father, a night watchman, we'd leave Long Beach

before daybreak, our binoculars scanning open water
for the ephemeral swordfish fin or pod of dolphins.

This is where he felt closest to his father, gone
before I was born. They'd wait, listing in the rocky

diesel scented tuna tower, listening for the zip of the lines,
praying for the splash, the yanking of rods, the yelling

for the captain to spin the boat around, gaffing the big one,
then slamming her down on the deck. The fish arching

and gasping in the sun, its body, their victory, something
impossible they'd pulled off together, conquering

the expanse of an ocean. Masts flying with triangles
of tuna, skipjack and marlin, as the sun lost hold,

I know what he must have felt as they pulled into harbor—
I knew, standing beside him on the bridge, floating

in that wordless adrenalin as we trailed into dock, the two
of us looking down on the circus of blood and pelicans.

Lost Between La Garita and La Paz

There are horses
on this freeway, Mexico 19,
and roses in the backseat

of the car and they're rambling
in the wind like somebody
on acid, petals cutting lose

like purple butterflies.
At a table at Tre Galline
last night a guy sang

a song he wrote about
transients. I know
something about this,

having been one.
He sang about Freedom
with a Capital F

for Fuck, for Frio and Feliz,
for Fantasmagórico,
those ants, so small

you think you're imagining,
F for Frightened
by packs of dogs, their balls

hanging as they roam
this street—the night,
a long cave, a color

so dark most have never
seen it, what it is to worry
about where you'll sleep,

and what it's like to not
worry about paying rent
and the fear

that if your car flips,
it'll take a while
to find you on this road,

if they ever do like the bull
ditched to the shoulder,
his sturdy horns

the only part protected
from maggots
and buzzards. And I

picture myself roadside.
What will be left of me,
as Mexico City sinks

since we drank so much
of its water, leaving
little to keep it afloat.

Whale Anthem

In a low inflatable boat
after the sun fell
off Land's End, in Cabo,
sitting in the wet Zodiac,
we heard it, wavering—

muffled like music
on the other side of a wall
or maybe miles away,
an echo. The timbre hit
my chest before my ears,

pulsing my body like a kick drum.
From a microphone lowered
fifteen feet into the sea came
the psalm of sorrow and relief,
someone making love

or dying—the throb of longing,
a sustained heartbeat, maybe
the womb. I couldn't listen
for long, the expression
of unretrieved emotion,

lovelorn like wolves in a cave
calling the moon. The whale's Om
dissolved into foghorn drone.
A friend sent me a video
of a whale swimming to the lip

of his little boat tilting to one side
as he coaxed her, pleading
Gracias Corazon, gracias Corazon
until she rose from the water
and he reached for her face.

I've heard their skin, covered
in lice and lesions feels muscular,
smooth as a peeled hardboiled egg.
I can't shake the purr, that chorus,
alto sax and oboe, above and below,

sounds spilling into one another,
the same long moan as when
I lost my mother, when my children
were born, the song I hum
sometimes alone in the dark.

Cuerpo

I wanted to tell you about the shifting light,
how marigold spread across both ends of the sky
after the sun set here between the Sierra de la Laguna

Mountains and the ocean 7,000 miles from Brisbane.
Instead, I am writing about a dead child
in the back of a small white car that pulled over

to help, the driver on his way to a funeral home
in Cabo. I want to explain how I fell to my knees
struggling in the deep sand after our car stalled

an inch from a cliff, want to write about how
not an hour earlier your body blanketed mine
against a rock jetting over the water, how

the ground trembled later when I stood
on the starless freeway waving for help
from disinterested truckers flying past

my flailing arms—just some crazy gringa
with a dog on an unlit dirt road between
two small Mexican towns while you stayed back

with the car. I could go on about the satellite
skimming the Milky Way, how you looked at me
under the half-lit moon and asked, *Is this too much,*

and I said yes. But all I can think of is what was under
that sheet, not how I had packed a picnic and we
only ate three grapes or how my skin became braille

under your hands, and I wanted to escape the earth
even before I knew what was in that backseat. I won't
go on, how impossibly we scaled the rocks

and startled at the screaming surf, how we traipsed
down in near darkness, sharp granite grazing
my bare feet. I can't write about the cold wind

and your warm mouth, the stars bright as headlights
so far from the city, how I had to pee in the sand,
how embarrassed I was though the waves drowned

out the sound, flummoxed, when the driver told me
what he was carrying, he and his co-worker stopping
anyway to shove our car to safety, how I gunned

the gas flinging rocks and dirt into their faces
as they pushed us in their white suits and funeral
home nametags until all of us were covered in dust.

The Visitor

Not sure I've ever seen her, but the dog food bowl
is empty this morning and her fresh dark prints
paint the white wall out back. She jumps down

at night. I may have seen her once on the hill,
a wild cat, tail thick as a squirrel's, color of
the mountain. I think of her on Tuesdays at 2pm

as the women play dominos near the pickleball court,
their faces reflected in pickleball-blue, laughing
and chatting. Alone on my balcony, I imagine her

perched over the roofline staring down at me,
eavesdropping on Tchaikovsky, Piano Trio
in A Minor. I think about her clawing her way

in her refuge of rocks above the Pacific, slipping
into my kitchen for leftovers, wandering
ledge to ledge in total darkness or torrential

rain or brazen daylight, chasing mice
over jagged edges, the sun darting orange
light into her eyes. No one will know

whether she survives the season, until enough
time passes that someone like me looking up
at the mountain will notice she's no longer there

sprinting from rattlesnake to scorpion, deft,
on her own to find water in the desert, the low
amber moon's heavy crescent on her back.

Between Long Beach and Catalina

My father tied a harness
             around my waist so I could
                 reel in
the dorado. I watched his steady hands,

          boat and fishing pole see-sawing
             in his sunglasses,
                 like a film
in fast forward, as scales splattered

          the deck, jewels at my feet—
             shins splashed with salt,
                 blood and victory.
I never felt more loved than when I'd find

          a swordfish a quarter mile out
             or hook a tuna
                 on my own.
I'd breathe in his afternoon cloud

          of diesel, scotch and cigarettes
             as he'd show me off
                 to his friends,
a pretty girl who could land a fish.

Why I Get Anxious Crossing the Street

I've been afraid that if she could fall
like that, so could I, so could everyone
I love, so could every person I see
on the street, all of us. I've felt

like a bird without feathers crossing
Wilshire Boulevard, in danger driving
down quiet back roads, walking up steps,
stepping on flat sidewalk. Everywhere

it seems there are reminders, a sign
in LA, Franklin, the name of her street
in New York. A homeless woman
in the alley yesterday stooped to look

at her belongings, plastic grocery bags
filled with things, like she was evaluating
what to keep, what to ditch, just as I've
bent in front of my closet deciding

what to keep, what to ditch. Still, no one
told me this would happen, that something
terrible will happen. So, I'm telling you.
And I am sorry. And you're welcome.

Exploring Hunger In Two Parts

I
Half a toasted banana muffin, a handful
of blueberries, pineapple and Nespresso—
  It's 7am on the porch

and you're trying to make yourself
   eat.
You're the fish that won't take the bait;

your lips sewn shut. Your mother said,
  Never eat bread. You binged
on Ex-Lax in college and saw

   a fat girl in the mirror
till your weight dropped
like rocks off a cliff, your belly

lassoed, strangled like a bull,
   down to 85 pounds.
Your parents took you

   to a shrink. You learned
to stomach three meals a day
and bury the scale in the yard,

though eating is still like stuffing
   a fork down your throat
or a long hose attached to the sewer.

   You don't want to bother,
go to the trouble of putting
pickles on a plate,

to worry about what's coming,
the next meal,
   to keep the body

alive, for what, another day
watching waves
        thrash the sand,

to hear the same yellow bird
        bitching
in the almond tree.

II
The same bird is bitching
        in the almond tree.
You're watching the waves

        thrash the sand
and you're eating to keep your body
alive. Some days you don't want to

bother, go to the trouble,
to put pickles on a plate,
        to worry about

what's bugging you, the next meal.
Eating's like stuffing a fork
        down your throat,

a long hose attached to the sewer.
        A shrink convinced you
to stomach three meals a day

and bury the scale in the yard.
        You dropped
to 85 pounds, rocks off a cliff,

        belly strangled
like a bull, a fat girl standing
in the mirror, her lips sewn

shut. Your mother said,
Never eat bread. So, you are trying
to make yourself

swallow.
You're the fish that won't take
the bait. You force-feed a handful

of blueberries, pineapple, half
a banana muffin and coffee
on the porch. It's only 7am.

When the Waiter Says I Love You

I'm walking off Wilshire where olive trees
are goddesses. Some have exposed roots
the size of shrubs. I threw my arms around
a waiter at the restaurant last night. Some have
bark, smooth and wrinkled like human skin.
The waiter whispered *I love you* in my ear.

One tree's limbs intersect like her own arms
are wrapped around her body. These trees
are beloved, like the cherry trees my Ex
planted for each of us that grew tall, flowered
pink in summer until the marriage ended
and new owners ripped them out like weeds,

easy as pulling silverware from a dishwasher,
or more like the bully who pulled my ponytail
in third grade. Some limbs clutch their angry
hands. You can't really own a tree. You can't
keep a tree from being happy or beautiful
like ones I climbed as a girl. There at the top

of my front yard sycamore on Carmelina
with its patchwork skin, I was safe on its wide
branches from the shouting in the kitchen,
and later as an adult, when I climbed the rungs
drenched in magnolia, towering, I remembered
on Stanford Street where palms look like pineapples,

their trunks topped in dreadlocks. The trees see
everything on this street. Some have leaves like
Mondrian's Red Tree, its trunk bloody, branches
raven. I'd love to live in a birch, or with one
in the middle of a room, like Van Gough's Mulberry
Tree, alive and unkempt, with fistfuls of raspberry

and saffron. In Hollywood, Italian cypress cathedral
the hills. The reception desk at Hotel 1 is made of a single
Aleppo pine. In Santa Monica, one canopy looks like the tip
of a paintbrush dipped in gold. Crows rest rigid atop a naked
tree. Some saplings are dying. When I am scared, I look
at the forest from up high and think I can see God. It felt

good to hear *I love you,* though I knew it meant nothing.
These trees stand by me, steadfast as I walk thinking
about last night, wondering what would happen if
everyone told a stranger they loved them. Here,
on Washington Avenue a valley oak trunk with the
furrowed face of an old man leans toward me as I go.

Hunting for Wild Mushrooms

We walked miles but saw no morels,
         only ticks on the dog's paw,
another under my right breast.

We found a lemon peel, poison ivy,
         a half-buried baseball cap
and orange surveyor's tape

wrapped around a water oak,
         a reminder of how much
we want, when what we search for

we cannot find, like when I left
         my former life, the lids
I forgot to take to go with the pots,

drawers large enough for sweaters,
         the old closet big enough
for a real vacuum. I lumbered past

so many without seeing, thinking
         them toxic, honeycombed
clumps. But we gathered rocks

dressed up in frog-colored moss,
         handfuls of pinecones
the size of silver nickels, baby blue

lichen, and clusters of pine needles
         bursting like sparklers.
The next day at dusk,

in my mycophilia, we found one,
         a morel the size of a brain,
golden in Sunday light, then ten

in the same flat field under
         green elms. Dirt beneath
my nails, I cupped the fragile

fungi like a newborn bird,
         color of a faded daffodil,
smelling of truffle and swamp.

Last Quarter, Void of Course Aquarius Moon

Soft-shoeing down Peachtree Street
between bulldozer dust and the din
of angry traffic, another wreck

in front of my loft, skid marks in circles
on the street, track marks on my arm
from the surgery, as I track violence—

spa shootings on Piedmont Road,
racing and road rage on I-20. Angst
melts on my tongue with fig gelato,

my hand smelling of salmon
and jalapeño since the Velvet Taco
doesn't offer forks unless you ask.

Little is provided anywhere unless
you ask. And if you ask, you are
asking for it, *Greedy bitch.* I imagine

a marshmallow poker poking through
my heart. For so long I lived like the last
tree in a ruined forest, like the Joplin record

my father snapped over his knee,
like a mouth, red-lipped and rough
in Georgia Clay, reminding me

of its opposite. As I think of the lights
of Calabria at dusk across the Straight
of Messina from Taormina, like dancers

waltzing on a shiny stage, I come back
to the homeless man laid out in the sun
in front of me here on Peachtree

on this the first warm day of spring,
his arms overhead in repose, Buddha
smile on his lips, his skin rich

     as the night, one shoe on, the other
     leg crossed, barefoot and tapping
     to a song I will never hear.

El Farallón

*...a rock-like formation in the high part or cleft that protrudes
into the sea, near a coast...*
—Definición De Etimología

The horizon is kerosene—It is my skin flayed
to bone. It is a tangerine carrot separating day

from night. This is the same water I prayed to
as a girl. There were my painted toenails,

the yellow house I grew up in, the sun I watched
plunge the sea. I am back again to this vantage point

where I live on a hill in Baja, married
to an ocean that contains my father because

this is where we fluttered his ashes. This
is where my mother collected oil slick skeletons

and feathers for her paintings after the Valdez spill.
I can see aqua from every window. Even my lungs

are 83 percent water. I put the over-ripe tomatoes
on the stove with a garlic clove drenching them

in leftover Merlot as I notice the ocean disappear
again. I live by its giant mirror. At night, the wind

pours over my skin like silk scarves. At dawn,
exhausted from lingering, I want more of it—

more of that breeze, and waves as I clocked them
erasing my father, spilling his cinders like down

feathers until he was nothing, yet made of sailboats
and the shimmering scales and pescados he caught—

the pleading fisheye, pouting shark mouth, the sierra
spines and blood that wallpapered his boat. These days

cruise ships flush their waste tanks twelve miles out,
half-way between here and the horizon. This is home—

the kelp and current, the ballenas and buried
treasure, carcasses an inch below the surface

reminding me how little I know of living—
reminding me of the distance between one

emptiness and another, that it is too late
to die young. The calm tide, like fingers, thrums

the land, wafting pebble sized shells in jagged
lines, the same shape as the scar on my right palm.

And all I want is to climb the old stone steps
to Hotel Finisterra where Hemingway drank whiskey

and soda on the rocks above this beach, where
my father made O's with his smoke. And every day

waves hurry to beach themselves, to wash
the shore clean and leave behind what they must.

For the Shell-Less

I found a forum on how to treat snails
           with cracked shells and how they
can't go on without their curled container.
           One sympathist whose snail

           was barely alive, fed her cucumber
and sprayed her with water; page after page
           of fondness for the shell-less
and the caregiver alike. The creature lived

a while. And I call that bravery, while I am afraid
           of a red spot on a tooth near my gum,
afraid lethargy means I am dying of something.
           So I drive along the coast and watch

           waves wash water snow-cone blue,
a barbed wire fence bordering a tollbooth
           separating our car from the slums.
I pass a lion colored dog, dead in the road.

Abandoned cars—chipped and broken-fendered,
           window-shattered and mannequined
on the other side. The houses are made
           of scrap metal, doorways gaping

           like mouths. And someone is blaring
music on a radio and someone is drying
           a T-shirt on a pole and it's waving
like a flag, and a man and a boy are walking

with a fishing rod. But I can't tell whether
           they are on the road next to me
or the other side with the birds who go on
           singing like nothing is happening.

Doctor Good

I've seen him take a fishing hook
out of a man's cheek, diagnose
a bikini-clad woman on the beach

where she sat with her son—his form
of flirting. My father rarely came home
before bedtime to sink into scotch

and a spy thriller, shut off from me
in his Salem cigarette smoke, leaving
early in his scent of Dial soap. After

my parent's split, he detailed how a date
wrapped herself in cellophane and ribbon
to answer his knock. I wondered if that

was the trick to being loved. He was
a charmer, all sunlight, bravado, rod
and reel, binoculars affixed to his face

in his suntan, making margaritas
and fresh caught dorado dressed in salt,
and mayo. A poor boy from Long Beach,

builder of boats, scrubber of decks, spent
from the line of patients who'd fly in
to see him, the one I blamed when I ran

away and sat under a purple orchid
tree hoping he'd find me, or at least
come looking. And yet, I would find

my way back to the ocean, his presence
all around in the afternoon sky, filled
with turkey vultures and sea mist.

What My Father Taught Me

He is standing in the hall,
framed by a walnut mopstick

banister, a vinyl valise
over his shoulder. He is tall

and elegant in his suit,
his thin black hair slicked back.

I wonder if he knew I sat there
on the third stair in my striped

slacks and peace sign pendant
listening to the arguing, wondering

if he packed toothpaste or a razor.
Did he bring a raincoat or shoes

for dancing. How many pairs of socks?
I couldn't know, sitting in the gold

shag carpet if he had everything
he needed. Did he forget his watch?

Did he pack his alarm clock? His
Old Spice cologne, the cigarettes

I had never seen him without? Did he
take a stethoscope for hospital rounds,

his belt, the navy and white dot
tie I gave him for Father's Day?

The overnight case with the zipper?
And I wondered then as I do now,

was he trying to teach me
to carry a heavy bag of my own.

My books press their bodies,

one on top of another,
Women Icons of the 20th Century
on the bottom bearing the weight

of it all. *Portraits* above.
The Matisse paintings topple out
by themselves, pages which belonged

to my grandmother Lena who kept it
on her yellow crocodile end table
in the den. Part of its spine has split,

tattered by curious fingers—
much like me. My mother's *Collected
Works* floats on top in its shiny, new

post-mortem purple and royal blue,
as pinkie-width feathers keep slipping
from pillows and the couch. I found

one on the stove, another on the floor
near my bed. It's like they're looking
for a better place, out the window,

twisting six floors down to land
in another universe on a bench, beside
a girl who might believe it's a sign.

A Witness to Solitude

The Mexican almond tree changes its leaves
like a cardigan from green, to freckled,
to copper. I used to wonder if it counted—

watching the sun shrivel and purr,
like I couldn't hold a memory by myself.
This morning, my dog in the other chair

as boats stream across the choppy sea,
smacking over whitecaps, their long Om,
one's small lamp visible in the early light.

Under the shifting sky a fly buzzes, barely
audible, the air neither hot nor cold. I can hear
leaves on the palm separating, the ixora renya's

blood-red eyes open in the thaw of day, all this
life spread out around me, the grass like razors,
the feral cat waiting for a neighbor's handful.

Near Diamond Mountain, Calistoga, CA

The night brought flames,
helicopters and planes fighting fire.
Walls of it circled the wood room

where I lie awake under a cathedral
ceiling, beside plyboard bookshelves
after it took down the main house.

Fire engulfed the forest,
the oak, elderberry and maple,
licking trunks black.

I could hear them falling, a rush
like a waterfall in the distance.
The ones still towering at sunup

were bloodied soldiers frozen
in their step, the lucky and alive,
like this brittle clapboard

patio I stand on, though it screams,
Burn me! as the birds weave
nests out of singed leaves.

My Father's Ashes

I have his brown eyes and dark skin.
I do not have his certainty, his calm
demeanor in crisis, his thin legs.
I have his ashes in my hands, fine,
like dust, except for the pieces
of bone we give back to the sea.

Mad at the Moon

Loitering and bald, pock-marked,
       ignorant, illiterate,
dressed in stones, distant, strange,
       always alone,

240 thousand miles off,
       no one wants to hang out
with the moon. You can't
       breathe there.

Worthless moon, invisible by day,
       then using someone
else's light. Irrelevant and old—
       there is no point.

It just hovers there, no use
       to anyone. It doesn't sing
or take out the trash. It has never
       read Shakespeare

or changed a tire. If I could, I would
       rip it out of the sky. It only
stood there glowering the night
       my father put metal

to his mouth, silent again, it
       observed through a window
as my mother fell, watching,
       doing nothing, static

and stuck. The moon can't
       get off its ass—like now
glistering the water with foolish
       sparks of light.

Cabo San Lucas, Independence Day

I've become this odd person,
sneaking in and out of my own home,
drinking wine with cereal

for dinner in a room I built off the garage,
so I can live here while renting out my house.
The rental company said, *Be invisible.*

I understand invisible, like when I was married,
and now I am again, or trying to be. If I saw
the renters, I'd duck. I eat bananas

with milk and Raisin Bran all day
since going to the market would be noisy.
I am forgetting things, the keys,

where's my phone, perhaps on account
of being so freaked out, preoccupied
with hiding. I leave cabinet drawers

open slightly to avoid the click, push
apart glass doors like a thief, scold the dog
for barking. Her anti-barking collar

isn't working. I hear a chair skid
across my ceiling. Surely, they can hear
my faucet. I'm trying not to clang

the spoon against the cereal bowl,
wear socks, step lightly, no blow-dryer.
It's an obsession, radio volume low,

napkin under a wineglass, careful
stacking plates, muffle a sneeze,
don't flush, whisper to the dog.

And when my chair honks the floor,
I picture the renters freezing
where they stand, listening

like my life depends on shutting the fuck up,
depends on being voiceless. Like I was
never here, like I'm already gone.

Going Down for the Third Time Today

On the elevator, a woman hears me sigh. She says,

me too. I say, *mine's worse.* I'm shallow and competitive

even in ICU around all this dying. I fold my mother's red

and white shirt, sweater and sweats into her knockoff

Longchamp bag, street clothes now useless as rags,

beside the blue neck brace, the A-line in her artery,

the channels as hard to count as branches along the river.

When Grief Is Not a Gift

It was not a like a letter in the mail,
an invitation to be opened. It flew
in my door like a turkey vulture

swooping down on her prey. Sidestepping
was not an option any more than ignoring
a hurricane when it slams a brick

through your window sucking out everything
you own and chucking it into the sea. The grief
of losing her and the marriage and my home

during five weeks in May was not *a gift*
as I've heard some say. I do not believe it was
meant to be or for the best. Grief didn't teach

me about myself or that we are connected.
The dirt taught me that—I am no match
for the brutal conditions, unlike the towering

Cardon cactus who survives 110 degree summers
without a sip. One waves to me from the mountain
as I sit at its base near Todos Santos. One raises

her hand desperate and twisted as if begging.
Another offers the peace sign. One gives me
the finger, wild and covered with eyes. One

is bent reminding me how my father held
his arm around my shoulders. And a giant one
sleeps out my window like a noble ancestor.

200 years old and 40 feet tall, she says,
You have seen nothing. They are all crooked,
stumped and stuck, discolored from stress.

You can see the imprint of age and wounds
from too much or too little water, burns
from frost. With their wet and fleshy insides,

some die—and I wonder if they grieve too
as they reach their gnarled fingers
up to who knows where.

Hurricane Warning, Baja, CA

They've closed the harbor
on the flat, slate sea. The last lights
flicker off in the mist like tarnished
jewels. My dog is eating her own shit
today, and my disposable coffee cup
leaks from too many reuses. Finally,
I find my phone on top of a suitcase,
sat down to smash a cockroach.
The ocean is empty—like it's waiting,
the wind like a motorcycle revving.
I watch rain on the hill spiral down
on the other side of Baja, to wreak
havoc on someone else's town first.
Trolling back, I see half a bird's egg,
size of a penny on my front step.
I think of her, cracking free from her
marbled home, open mouthed, scrawny
and learning to fly, but into a storm,
and wonder will she survive the rain
that will come in sideways, the branches
flailing like a castaway, the smoky
pink clouds gathering on the horizon.

Letter from Summer in LA

You were alive, ageless and painting,
or wandering in LA's afternoon citrine,

air glittery on the harbor, boats barely moving
like a body breathing, like it was when we lived

on a bluff. Seasons blur. It's summer here
every day after the fog lifts. Muraled walls

in Venice have wings. Tattooed bikers
have taken over Front Walk. One year

since I saw you. Decades since we moved
out of LA. Remember the Hwy 10 tunnel

opening to the ocean, palm trees, hills draped
in brown, toupeed in green mops, that cliff

we'd hike near Chautauqua, the Santa Monica
Pier, sun setting at Gladstone's, the roses

and bottle brush trees that bloom all year,
your smock smelling like turpentine.

The Weight of Grief

Flip on the light switch,
rummage for the mustard jar
in the cupboard—everything
required great effort once
she was gone. The muscle

to grip and twist the cap.
The intention it took to peel
plastic from the lip. Drop it
in the trash, reach the shelf.
Take out a plate. The weight.

The debate, plate or lunch
on a napkin. Consider
the time to rinse the dish.
Open the dishwasher, gauge
where to stash the plate.

What it would require later
to remove it and stack it
in the cabinet. This simple,
not simple act of adding
condiment to pre-prepared

sandwich. The ache for a nap.
Once a week I'd wash my hair.
I fed myself and the dog,
put off more difficult things
like changing my name.

One thing at a time. The light,
the switch, the plastic, the jar,
the trash, the knife, the bread,
the cupboard, the napkin,
or the plate. The napkin.

Whale Watching, La Laguna San Ignacio, Mexico

The walking paths are crushed white shells
rattling like chains under your step
as wind wheezes through haggard palms

on this cold March morning. You're wearing
all your clothes, two t-shirts, three sweaters,
a windbreaker. At the Ignacio Springs B&B

they serve sweet lips fish for dinner, rosé
and Costco lemon pie. On the lagoon
today a grey whale steered her 40-ton body

to place her face in your hand, an inch
below her left eye, and you felt chosen.
Just 100 whales stay for now as the others go

to Alaska for the summer. A dozen came
to the panga, swimming around, beside
and beneath us, their babies, gliding

and rolling, mothers rubbing their barnacles
on the bottom of the boat as you trailed
your toes in the water idling, chosen.

And shells on the packed sand spiraled
into chandeliers, and on the long tope
filled dirt road back, you sailed, exhausted

from three days of travel, back to the owls,
roosters and stray dogs barking, the usual
out of town evening water sounds. You sleep

in a yurt, under a circus ceiling, beneath
blue and white flowered sheets listening
to the bed springs through your pillow.

And through the window you, chosen, watch
the moon cellophane the river as the last
of the green-winged teal splashes into night.

Hating Me for It

I left it up to her
        when to die, as if I had
        any choice in the matter.

I took La Bohème
        playing on my cellphone,
        and my raincoat and left

her alone in the hospital
        where she had been dying
        beside me long after

the white coats turned off
        the blinking machines.
        Now on her pullout couch,

springs against my back,
        half sleeping, I waited
        for the news, thinking

about our argument days earlier
        when she blared at me
        to leave. I agreed,

knowing in my gut I should
        have stayed. And I
        might have caught her,

and she'd be here now, sick
        as hell, aching maybe,
        and hating me for it.

My Mother's Nudes

They lean against the brick
    in my hallway, half-dressed
in heaps of bubbles, crêpe paper,

and humidity. Broken AC,
    in just a bra, I pose
her nudes around my place

surrounding myself with her
    dancing across my walls,
painting my room in acrylic

cologne, reminding me of Picasso
    who said, *there is a vial
of my blood* in each of these.

It's too late to protect them, strips
    of turquoise peeling from torsos.
She stacked them together, paint

on paint. Now preserved, sorted
    and catalogued, her Erotic Series,
bodies intertwined in tangles

of breasts, limbs and shadow.
    I wrap my face in museum-
grade plastic. The Dartek sucks

and seals my mouth, my nose
    and pores. Tomorrow
I'll begin to clean up our mess.

What's True

We buried my mother's ashes

We tossed her belongings
       into a dumpster

The boys moved away

A new owner bulldozed
       the ranch house

       surrounded by trees
The apartment kept flooding

We replaced the toilet
       twice

The AC broke

I curled on the floor

sobbing a couple days a week
       My girlfriend said

a branch not a fist
       blacked her eye

I wake up shaking
       My dog waits for me

on a cushion
       her tail dangling

like a fairytale

       A pipe froze behind a wall
and the drip took

       two weeks to find

We Were Happy Until
We Pretended We Were

I have learned not to believe
in trains, the hypnotic certainty

of steel clanging on rails. Now
I wear yoga clothes all day,

use a drugstore toothbrush
as a vibrator. I am wood.

I am a little mirror. I am
a book, bedside.

Self Portrait as Puppet

—After Hannah Hoch (1889-1978)

My mouth stitched shut
with orange thread.
Such a waist—
tied tight with silk rope.

A gift? My golden skirt
dangles, and I dance
when jostled, bangles

lock my knees. Puffy feet
go nowhere. Pointy breasts,
like the rest of me, wait here
on a string until a hand slips

inside me moving my mouth
to somebody else's words.
I am two-faced, yellow skin

on one side, bubblegum
on the other. Glassy brown
eyes shine though I cannot
see or cry, or scream.

Behind the Armoire at Tienda 17

His tongue, a mango slice

inside my mouth. Eyes, slate

clouds. Arms, the sun.

Hair, feral. Jaw, pepper

and sandpaper. His breath,

my breath. We are running

out of days.

Some Drunks

I have heard there are drunks
who fall asleep in their clothes
on the couch in the living room,

who flirt, and slur, and smell
like gin. I've heard some say
I'm sorry in the morning

and scuffle down halls keeping
their fists in their pockets.
Some eat all the powdered

sugar dusted donuts, they want
Cartier, and they sing too loud
with friends. Some drunks do

not shout *fuck you* at people
they love. I've heard some die
or get sober and come home,

placing their suitcases back
on the upper shelf quietly
because you are asleep.

But all I know is the morning sun
has turned the sky peach
and miles out, across

the Chattahoochee River, smoke
billows from a powerplant
drowning this valley in lavender.

Total Solar Eclipse, August 21

I am speeding toward totality
        under a ceiling cracking
        at my Atlanta apartment,

sitting on blue green zinnia upholstered
        chairs, steeping oolong as birds
        still breed and breathe.

Before the hummingbirds come,
        the ants. I crush the small ones
        with my lemon scented sponge.

Monday lunges by like this shadow
        speeding toward us, like the trial
        to erase our vows, like my mother's

decline. For two minutes and 40
        seconds, the moon swallows
        the sun. Then we crawl back

into glistering haze. I hear my pulse
        quake, and wonder where
        on my body shall I put my hands?

Something to be Thankful For

Grateful for the long swim to shore
that nearly did me in, for the smallest
rock on the widest beach, the bite
in the center of a peppercorn, filament
in a light bulb, the rush of blood
in the veins, the echo after a wave,
the long hum of a fishing boat
on the Pacific, the sensory memory
of a basil farm when he opened
the car door to leave, the way a leaf
still shudders after the wind, how my legs
ache while climbing the steep front steps,
for the water that leaks under
my front door, flooding my foyer, grateful
for the floor, the flood, the rain, the recycled
glass bowl that holds paint, for the brush
and sandpaper to repair the damage,
grateful for grief, for the pain and reprieve
from it, the dulling that time brings,
for being tired, for sleep and waking,
for the mountains in Baja, green after storms
end a decade of drought, for the sound a horse
makes when she breathes, her knowing,
her length, and fragile legs, for the dog
who brings me ticks, for the woods, for cheap
champagne, for coffee so strong it tastes
like a cigarette, for cinnamon and the cold
lake melting like marmalade on my back,
for the way the seagull lifts her bill,
for the colors that streak her slate grey
beak, that today nothing hurts, but the cut
where my thumbnail meets the skin,
for the rare orange blossom in my garden
of stumps, grateful for torso and taste buds,

for the moonless night, for breaking
glass, for the smell of bacon burning
and the wingspan of clouds, how they
change from wispy to reptilian every day.

My Dead Father Comes Back
As a Brown Bird

Today a plain bird, in his brown
feathered vest, size of my father's
fishing reel, hit the glass with a thud
and landed in my open hall to rest

his caraway seed eyes on mine. He sat
near me, listening, bobbing his head
as I froze an inch away. I could almost
hear him breathe and I remembered

my father saying he'd come back
a sparrow, basic and nut brown.
And for the first time I talked to him, aloud,
thanking this small, stunned bird for making

me strong, till he hop-flew off, leaving me
sitting there on the cold tile, watching
as he wafted into the tree canopy outside,
the sound of geese cutting north for the season.

Acknowledgments

Many thanks to the editors who first published these poems, sometimes in different forms:

All Breathing Things Anthology: "Lentiformis Mensencephali"
Aji magazine: "Mad at the Moon"
Artemis Journal: "Whale Anthem"
Brickplight: "Between Long Beach and Catalina"
Cutthroat: "Going Down for the Third Time Today"
Green Hills Literary Lantern: "My Father's Father"
Hole in the Head Review: "My Books Press Their Bodies," "Last Quarter Void-of-Course Aquarius Moon"
La Presa: "Recuerdo"
Malibu Poetry Anthology: "Lentiformis Mesencephali"
Mudroom: "My Dead Father Comes Back as a Brown Bird"
Open: Journal of Arts & Letters: "Letter from Summer in LA," "What's True," "Behind the Armoire at Tienda 17," "Something to be Thankful For"
Pedestal Magazine: "El Farallón"
Pink Panther Magazine: "Wild Mushrooms"
Pier-Glass Poetry: "Some Drunks," "My Mother's Nudes"
Plainsongs: "Why I Get Anxious Crossing the Street"
Terminus Magazine: "Bats flood the sky here at dusk"
The Opiate: "The Striped Marlin We Set Free"
Tiger Moth Review: "Whale Watching," "The Visitor"
Tupelo Quarterly: "Cuerpo," "Doctor Good," "Elephant Tree," "When Grief Isn't a Gift," "East Cape, Baja CA"
Waxing and Waning: "The Nature of Monogamy," "Lost Between La Garita and La Paz"

CYNTHIA GOOD, for years a recognizable face on the evening news in Atlanta, is also a known women's advocate who launched two award winning women's business magazines, *Atlanta Woman* and *PINK;* both of which won awards for editorial and design. She is the author of eight books, two of them collections of poems including the chapbook *What We Do with Our Hands.* Her book *Vaccinating Your Child* won the Georgia Author of the Year award. Cynthia's poems have appeared in numerous journals including *Artemis, Awakenings, Book of Matches, Brickplight, Bridgewater International Poetry Festival, Brief Wilderness, Cutthroat, Free State Review, Full Bleed, Green Hills Literary Lantern, Hole in the Head Review, Main Street Rag, Maudlin House Review, MudRoom, Open: Journal of Arts & Letters, Outrider Press, OyeDrum Magazine, The Penmen Review, Pedestal Magazine, Pensive Journal, Persimmon Tree, Pier-Glass Poetry, Pink Panther Magazine, Poydras, South Shore Review, The Ravens Perch, Reed Magazine, Tall Grass, Terminus Magazine, They Call Us, Tupelo Quarterly, Voices de la Luna, Waxing & Waning* and *Willows Wept Review* among others. She received her MFA in Poetry from NYU. A mother of two grown sons, Cynthia lives in Mexico and in Santa Monica with her Havanese dog named Zuni.

Milton Keynes UK
Ingram Content Group UK Ltd.
UKHW030853131024
449481UK00005B/240